Willow The Wonder Pug: A Kaleidescope of Kindness.
By Gina Villarreal Arcediano. 2024.
Illustrated by Maru Salem-Vargas

ISBN: 978-1-962407-78-6 (Paperback)

To Acacia,
Your resilience, beautiful vibrance and love of animals inspires me.

And to Aliyah,
A giver and healer in the making with a heart that shines bright, you are loved.

For Daija Bear,
The spunky Pug who started it all. I will always honor my promise.

Willow
The Wonder Pug
A Kaleidoscope of Kindness

By Gina Villarreal Arcediano

Illustrated By Maru Salem-Vargas

Life is a beautiful rainbow in Willow's world.
Willow starts her day snuggling with her six-year-old bestie,
Grace. When she wakes up, she rolls on her back for big tummy
rubs patiently waiting for their morning ritual.

"Are you ready?" said Grace. Willow's curlicued tail wiggled excitedly. Grace clears her sleepy throat and in her big announcer voice shouts, "Willow the Wonder Pug!" Willow takes a running start and leaps off the bed racing to start her day.

ZOOM!
ZOOM!

The perfect little pug lives up to her big, bold, superhero name. Not only is she the ultimate zoomie queen, but she and Grace have a little secret. Grace can understand everything Willow says.

One night before bed as the two cuddled, Grace said, "Hey, Willow, my friend from school is coming over to play tomorrow.

I can't wait for you to meet her."

"Yippee!" exclaimed Willow.

The next day, Willow delightfully romped through the garden with her friends Layla, the French bulldog, and Mozart, the boxer. They wrestled and played tug-of-war excited for Grace to come home.

Suddenly, the front door swung open. Grace and her friend Luna ran through the house to the backyard.

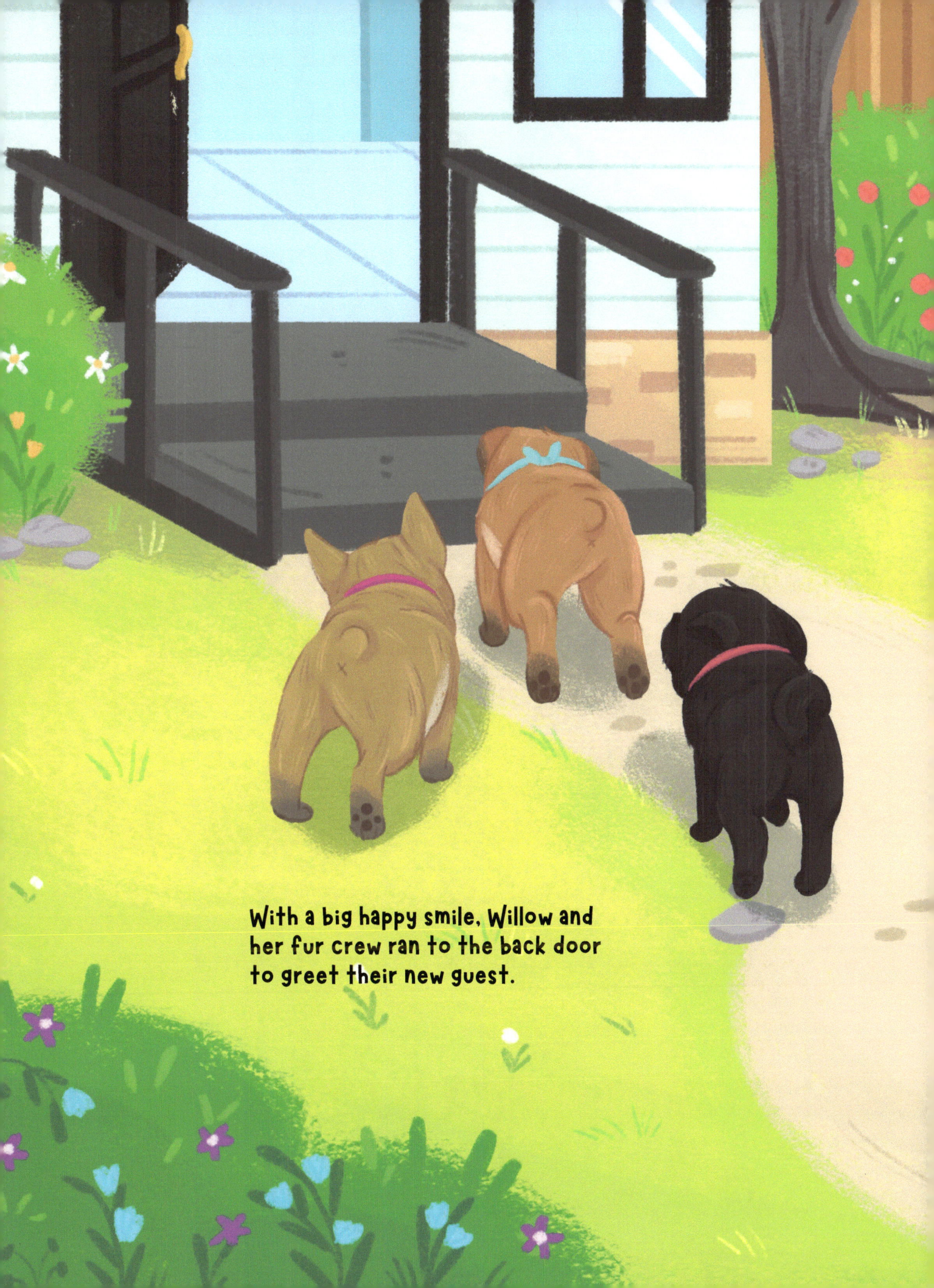

With a big happy smile, Willow and her fur crew ran to the back door to greet their new guest.

BONK!

Luna rattled the windows as she swung open the door, hitting little Willow in the face.

Willow barked, "Ouch, that hurt!"

Grace looked over in concern. She could see
Willow was in pain.

Layla and Mozart saw Luna coming
toward them like a whirlwind,
her curly pigtails flying through
the air.

Nervously, they tried to hide behind the flowers, pretending they were invisible. "Hi doggy, let's play horsey," Luna shouted as she waved her hands in Layla's face and tried to climb on her back.

Frightened, Mozart and Layla started to shake.
Their eyes bugged out in concern.

YEE HAW!

Grace ran across the yard, shouting, "Stop! Layla doesn't like that. You could hurt her."

OUCH!

"She's just a dog," Luna yelled as she excitedly turned her attention to Mozart, pulling his floppy ears from side to side. Mozart's teeth chattered. He knew he was supposed to be a brave boxer, but he crouched in fear.

Willow, frozen in panic, didn't know what to do. Suddenly, the gentle little pug remembered **HER VOICE.**

It was time to use her
Wonder Pug SUPERPOWERS.

Willow took a few deep breaths and found the courage to use her words.

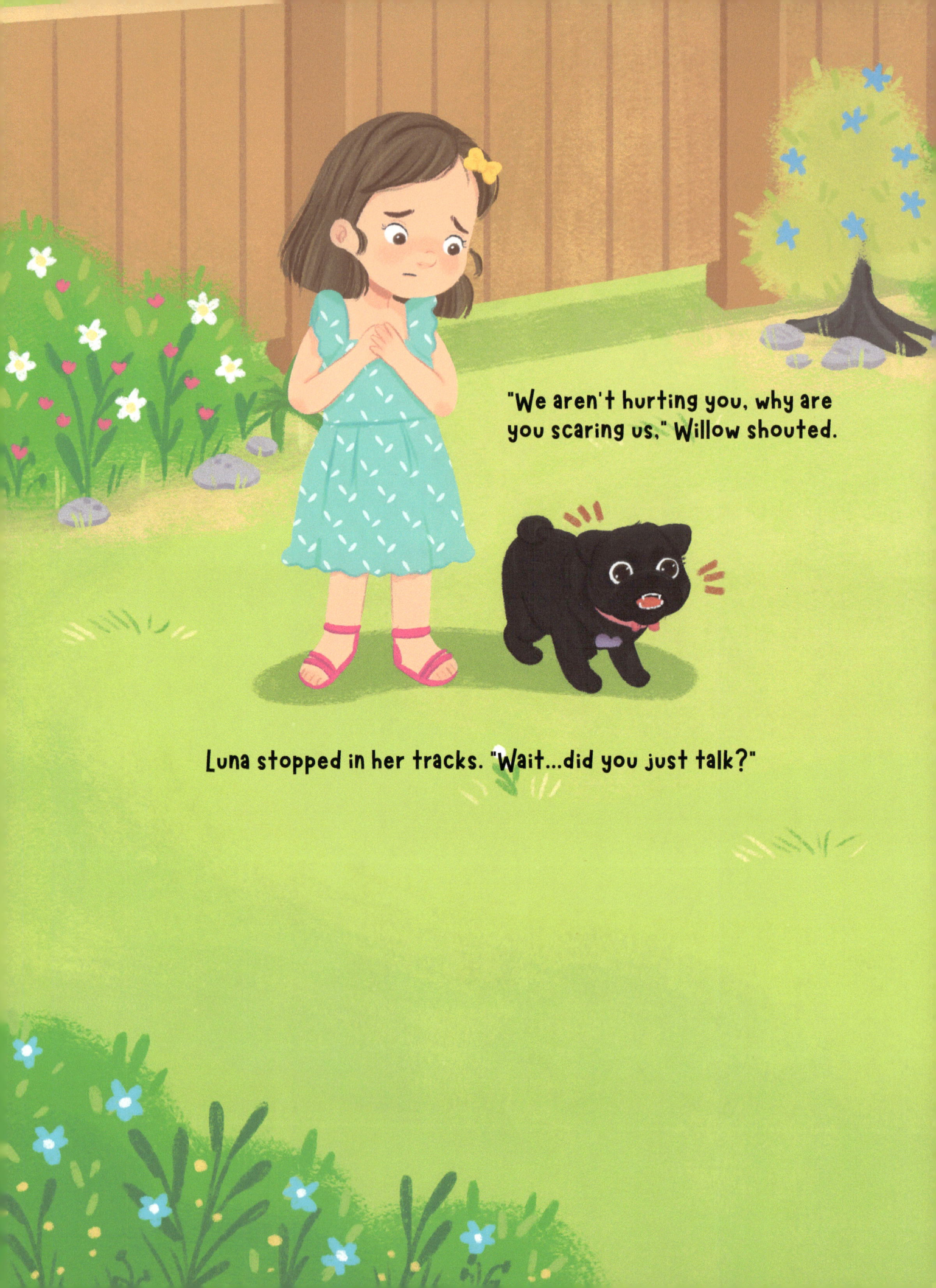

"We aren't hurting you, why are you scaring us," Willow shouted.

Luna stopped in her tracks. "Wait...did you just talk?"

"Yes," Willow said with confidence. "You wouldn't like it if I pulled your ears or jumped on your back, would you?"

Still stunned, the spunky 7-year-old said, "No, I guess not, but you're a dog. We can do whatever we want to you; you're just a pet."

"That is not true," Grace chimed in. "Animals have feelings too."

Willow and her crew walked over to the fence with a full view of the neighborhood. The Wonder Pug motioned to Luna, "Let me show you."

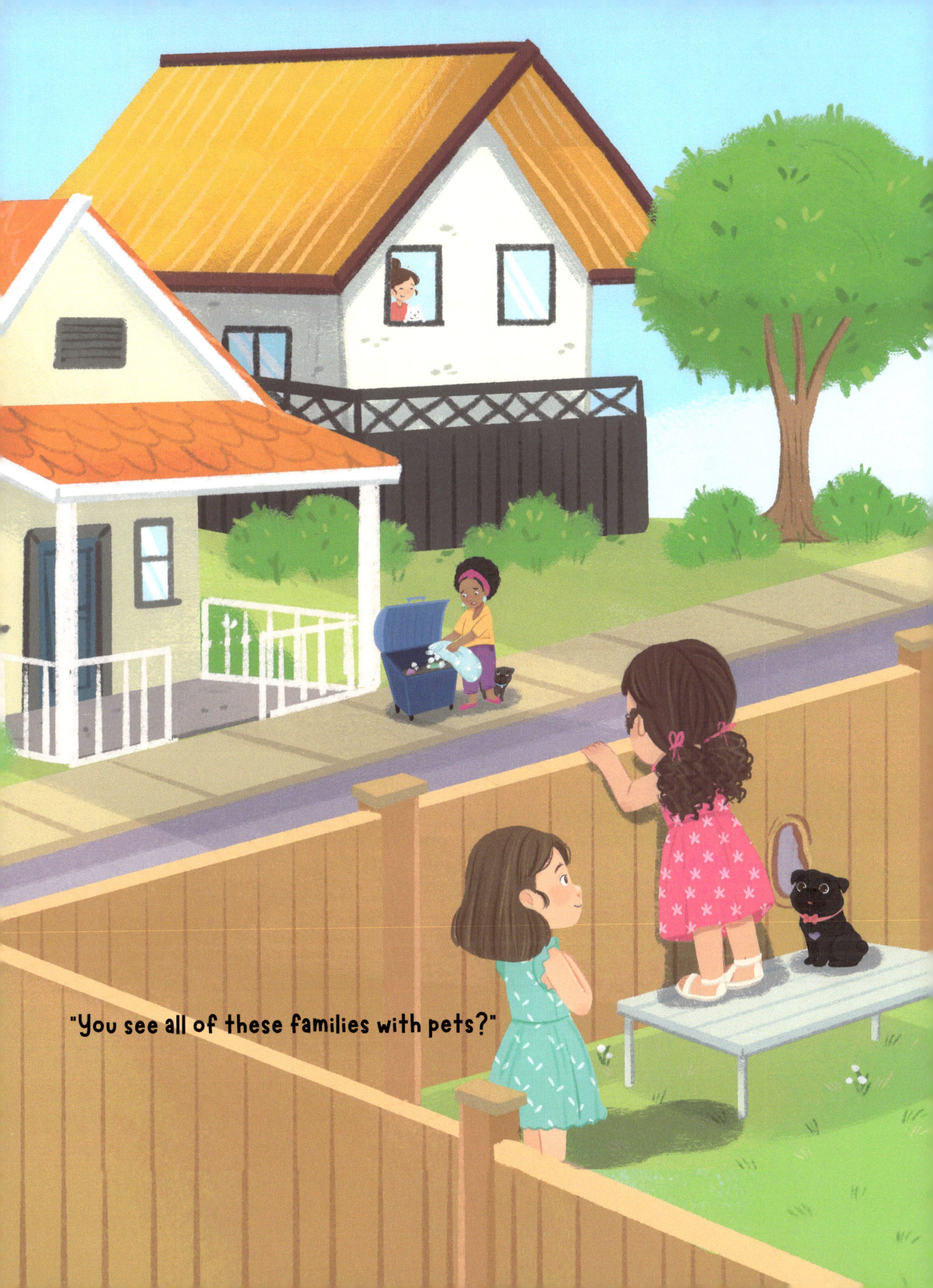

"You see all of these families with pets?"

"Look at my friend Bella, the Boston terrier over there...she's happy getting treats and belly rubs," Willow explained.

UGH!

Down the street, Bogey, the pug, walked with his head down behind his mom as she dumped the stuffing from the bed he destroyed in the dumpster.

"See him?" Willow gestured. "He's really sad. He got bored at home alone and made a messy mistake."

COWABUNGA!

"And check out my buddy Mooshu. He's a senior pug. His little human brother is chasing him and playing too rough, making him unhappy and scared"

"If you thought we couldn't feel pain, this definitely hurts." Willow showed Luna and Grace the bump that was growing on her forehead from the door hitting her face when Luna arrived.

"I didn't know animals should be treated with kindness," Luna admitted as she started to gently pet Mozart, Layla, and Willow.

"See how nice animals are when we learn how to treat them properly?" "You're my BFF (Best Friend Forever), and these little furballs are my best friends too," Grace explained.

HONK!
HONK!

Honk, honk. Luna's mommy was in the driveway to pick her up.

The girls skipped through the house. Willow, Layla, and Mozart followed.

Luna turned and said, "I'm sorry Willow. I'll never forget what you taught me today."

"Don't worry, now that you know, just remember, please treat people and animals the way you want to be treated."

Luna opened the door, greeted by a bright colorful rainbow peeking through the clouds.

"Look, Willow, a rainbow," she smiled.

"Wow!" Willow's deep brown eyes lit up.

Before Luna left the porch, Willow whispered to her, "Luna, I almost forgot to tell you, if others find out about my superpower..."

Luna giggled, "Don't worry Willow the Wonder Pug, you gave me a second chance today. Thank you for being the kindest, cutest pup I know."

The bright-eyed second-grader hopped in the car with enthusiasm, "Mommy, guess what? I'm going to share what I learned about animals at show-and-tell tomorrow so my friends at school will know how to treat animals with kindness."

Luna's mommy smiled. "What are you going to tell them?"

"I'm going to tell them I met Willow the Wonder Pug. I didn't know that animals have feelings. They are not just pets. They make us laugh, show us love, and bring us happiness. They really are family."

Hello from *Willow* The Wonder Püg

Hi Friends!
Guess What!? Luna went to school and shared everything she learned during her visit at my house.

I am very proud of her.

She told her class all about her new fur friends.

She Shared What She Learned:
All Animals Have Feelings
They Get Happy, Playful, Sad, Scared, Nervous and Sometimes Mad

When Meeting a New Pet

- We Always Approach Animals Carefully
- Ask for Permission Before Getting Close
- If Given Permission, Hold Out Our Hand & Let the Animal Sniff Before Petting.

To Learn More About Children & Pets
www.aspca.org/pet-care/dog-care/dogs-and-babies

Willow the Wonder Pug Wants to Hear from YOU!

She reads all of her special letters from readers just like you.

Tell Willow why you think she's a Wonder Pug?
What is your favorite part of the story?
Do you have a pet you want to tell Willow about?
Why do you think animal kindness is important?

Upload a Picture of You and Your "Willow the Wonder Pug" Book or Show Willow your Favorite Pet or Stuffed Animal.

*Willow may write back or say a very special hello to you on her website or social media.

Write to Willow: www.willowthewonderpug.com
Instagram: @willow_the_wonder_pug

ABOUT THE Author

Gina Villarreal Arcediano is a Latina Journalist & a creative visionary with a passion for storytelling. As a children's book author, Gina uses her extensive experience in media and public relations to create engaging, imaginative stories that captivate young readers.

As both a child and animal advocate, Gina's thought-provoking messaging and creative narratives, reflect her personal mission of giving a voice to the voiceless. Her stories not only entertain but also inspire children to dream big and believe in themselves. With every page, Gina & Willow hope to unleash their message of kindness and compassion, making a lasting impact on children world-wide.

TESTIMONIALS

"Willow the Wonder Pug is not just a story of a playful pup, but a heartwarming reminder of the bond we share with our pets. Through her gentle superpowers, Willow teaches us that animals, like people, have feelings and deserve kindness and respect. This is such a sweet tale of friendship, compassion, and second chances which shows how the smallest creatures can have a big impact on our hearts. A beautiful reminder that pets are not 'just animals' – they are family."
– Cristina Mendonsa, Award Winning Journalist & Filmmaker

Willow the Wonder Pug is a heartwarming story that teaches us how to be kind, loving, and caring to all living creatures. Willow has the unique ability to communicate which helps others understand how we can be more considerate to our pets and each other. Willow the Wonder Pug will be an amazing addition to any classroom library."
– Holly Harrigan, K–8 Visual Arts Teacher

"In a world that could always use more kindness, Willow the Wonder Pug shows us the transformative power of empathy, imagination, and love for animals. This story is a touching reminder that even the smallest voices can make the biggest impact in our hearts and lives."
– Ian Griffith, Transformational Leader & Bestselling Author